PURBECK POTTERY - A HISTORY & COLLECTORS' GUIDE

PETER FREEMAN AND ALAN PEAT

CREATIVE EDUCATIONAL PRESS LTD

PUBLISHED BY: Creative Educational Press Ltd, 2 The Walled Garden, Grange Park Drive, Biddulph, Staffordshire, ST8 7TA
Tel: 07789938923
Fax: 01782 379398

PRINTED BY: York Publishing Services, 64 Hallfield Road, Layerthorpe, York, YO31 7ZQ

Alan Peat   email: alanpeat@tiscali.co.uk   www.alanpeat.com

Peter Freeman   email: freed65@xtra.co.nz

ISBN: 978-0-9544755-9-8

Purbeck Pottery - A History & Collectors' Guide

CONTENTS

Since its founding in 1966 Purbeck Pottery has continually produced distinctive, high-quality ceramics. In the mid-1960s there was a developing appreciation of studio ceramics, which commercial pottery producers seized upon with enthusiasm. By 1966 both Denby and W.R. Midwinter Ltd had tableware ranges in production which owed a stylistic debt to the studio pottery movement. Purbeck was also at the forefront of this craft-pottery-influenced movement and the tableware produced by the company, with its highly vitrified stoneware body, lent itself well to this 'look'.

Longevity in a fickle marketplace has always been an indicator of quality. Purbeck's 'Portland' range has been in non-stop production for over forty years. In itself this is remarkable. However, it certainly does not indicate that Purbeck pottery is somehow 'frozen in time'. The long production life of Purbeck tableware is partially explained by the fact that it has gradually evolved through time – subtle changes in the hollowware handles provide an example of these gradual alterations. But success is also, undoubtedly, due to a uniqueness and individuality which affords Purbeck the 'design signature' which only the very best ceramic producers have ever achieved.

This Purbeck 'design signature' is most obvious in the highly textured decorative ware produced throughout the 1970s. This could not be mistaken for the output of any other pottery manufacturer; it is as distinctive as a thumbprint and it is this originality which makes Purbeck such an attractive proposition for the collector.

Purbeck is also of interest owing to the high quality of the personnel working for the company. Bob Jefferson, previously Head of Design at the nearby Poole Pottery, had an even more influential role at Purbeck. His Poole designs are already highly collectable and it is only a matter of time before his work for Purbeck follows suit. In addition, Eddie Goodall (previously

Senior Thrower at Poole) threw monogrammed vases (often clay-decorated by George Janes) for Purbeck, which are, today, a rare find.

Purbeck is also an exciting pottery to collect for those who admire pattern as well as form. Among the many collectable pieces are mugs with medieval decorations (reminiscent of Susan Williams-Ellis' work at Portmeirion); hard-to-find tankards with handpainted lustre decorations and pop-art-inspired, transfer-printed money boxes which are redolent of the late 1960s. One can even find 'flower-power'-inspired patterns on late 1960s mugs and saucers.

A 1967 article about Purbeck, in *Pottery Gazette and Glass Trade Review* concludes with the comment,

"By the time a visitor leaves Purbeck Pottery, a little of the enthusiasm of directors and workpeople alike has brushed off on him".

It is our hope that, with the production of this design history and collectors' guide, a little of the authors' own enthusiasm for this distinctive and remarkable pottery will have 'brushed off' on our readers.

Alan Peat and Peter Freeman

July 2011

"By the time a visitor leaves Purbeck Pottery, a little of the enthusiasm of directors and workpeople alike has brushed off on him."

POTTING IN PURBECK: AN HISTORICAL CONTEXT

The abundance of a quality source of clay found in the Wareham basin has been exploited by the people of this region over many centuries, eventually leading to the development of a significant pottery industry. The fine particle size, and hence high plasticity of the local clay, combined with a low iron oxide content which results in near white firing, has meant that the Isle of Purbeck has been the focus of continuous pottery production from the late Bronze Age through to the present day. The success of this industry has ebbed and flowed over the years in line with socio-economic trends and issues that have affected the locality as well as the nation as a whole.

Historically the Dorset pottery industry can be divided into a series of clear historical phases:

The Bronze Age (c.2100-700 BCE)

The Bestwall Quarry site near Wareham provides an exciting glimpse into the daily life of a Bronze Age settlement. Among the nationally important finds are rare examples of domestic beaker pottery from the Early Bronze Age, ceremonial pottery drinking sets from the Middle Bronze Age (c. 1400–1100 BCE) and extensive evidence of pottery production from the Late Bronze Age. The pottery was hand-built using a ring-building technique, a variation on a coil pot, without the use of a wheel. These would have been fired in clamps, which were basically shallow pits in which a fire had been laid and burnt down to embers. The pots were then placed on the embers and allowed to dry and heat through before being covered with further wood and finally covered with earth and left for twenty-four hours.

The Iron Age (c. 700 BCE-43 CE)

The people who populated the region at this time were members of the Durotrigian tribe, the name given to the people of Dorset prior to the Roman conquest. The pottery made at this time used the local ball clay and sands. It was also hand-built and finished by brushing the surface of the pot with a bone polisher. The resulting pottery is known as 'Black Burnished Ware' by archaeologists due to its coloration and finish. The Bestwall Quarry site has shown evidence of Middle Iron Age pottery production as well as earlier Bronze Age production.

The Romano-British Period (43–410CE)

The Durotrigian pottery industry survived and thrived after the Roman conquest of 43CE. They supplied their 'Black Burnished' pottery as general cookware to the legions and gradually the pottery was used throughout Roman Britain. Large quantities have been found in the Midlands, around London and as far North as Hadrian's and the Antonine Walls. The post-invasion Purbeck potters eventually adapted to the new styles that the Romans brought with them, copying favourite shapes, whilst still retaining the distinctive black burnished look, often decorated with simple sgraffito patterns consisting of geometric shapes and swirls. Romano-British potteries have been excavated at Arne, Corfe Castle, Corfe Mullen, Milton Abbas and Studland. At Bestwall over thirty firing pits have been uncovered dating from the Romano-British phase showing that pottery production was a major economic feature of the local area.

The Middle Ages (600-1500CE) and beyond

Following the collapse of the Roman Empire and the withdrawal of the Roman army, the national pottery industry at Purbeck seems to have reverted to the manufacture of wares for local consumption. This situation remained constant throughout the Middle Ages and there is ample documentary and archaeological evidence which demonstrate that a sustained local pottery industry was functioning.

Local pots had a variety of uses beyond the cooking of food. In churches they were used for acoustic purposes, such as amplifying the priest's voice during sermons. In the Churchwardens' Accounts of Wimborne Minster for 1541 the following entry can be found; "Payd for 2 potts of cley for wyndfyllyng of the Chyrch, 8d". An example of these early 'microphones' can be seen in the church at Tarrant Rushton which still has two pots set into the chancel-arch wall.

As stated before, this period of Dorset pottery history was very much based on a locally produced/locally consumed model, with perhaps a potter in each village supplying the local area's needs. Designs of local wares were influenced by imported wares, which the local artisans would interpret and replicate.

This situation changed with the introduction of 'tobacco' to the country.

The clay from the Wareham basin proved ideal for use in clay pipes and was in great demand. The trade actually became so successful that by 1749 complaints were made that the masters of ships loading pipe clay at Poole were jettisoning their ballast overboard and clogging up the vital navigation channels. Although the clay proved to be an important export opportunity, the tobacco pipe factory located in Wareham also provided the local populace with the necessary tools for partaking in the habit!

In the 18th century the quality of the local clays of Purbeck were acknowledged more widely. In 1720 the first Dorset ball clay arrived in the Staffordshire Potteries and in 1763 Josiah Wedgwood produced his Queen's Ware made from "the whitest clays of Devonshire and Dorsetshire, mixed with ground flints, and covered with a vitreous glaze".[1] So successful was this new thinner-walled pottery that in 1771 Wedgwood signed a contract with Thomas Hyde of Arne for the supply of 1400 tons of ball clay, thereby ensuring his place as England's leading potter.

1855 saw the establishment of the Patent Architectural Pottery in Hamworthy, boasting such products as coloured and glazed bricks and encaustic tiles among its extensive range of wares. Other manufacturers exploited the suitability of the local clays for this type of industrial pottery, amongst them Jesse Carter who, with his sons Charles and Owen, established what is today known as Poole Pottery. The gradual shift from industrial to domestic ware re-established Dorset as a major potting force which rivalled Staffordshire in both output and quality.

More recent developments include Sir John and Lady Bowland's establishment of the Purbeck Decorative Tile Co.

in Swanage in the 1950s. Their concept was to produce decorative tiles to order to fulfil the requisites of their customers' projects. They used screen-printing and employed designers such as Reginald Till to create their ranges. By 1959 the company had relocated to Newbury, Berkshire. It was taken over in 1984 before a final move to Clapham, London, where it ceased trading in the 1990s.

This historical tradition of pottery manufacture was continued by Christopher Russell who started a small studio pottery in Swanage in the 1950s. He named this 'Purbeck Pottery' and produced finely thrown, tin glazed stoneware *(Illus 1)* before becoming involved in the start-up of a pottery and arts centre

in Barbados. In 1965 Lucien Myers described Russell's work in *Design* magazine: "He decorates tiles with unusual and striking glaze effects, fused glass and metals, to create both pictorial and abstract panels.".[2]

In this article he is mentioned alongside such notables as Kenneth Clark, Alan Wallwork and Kenneth Townsend. He was also responsible for supplying ceramic tiles for decorative purposes at Swanage Library, which opened in 1965.[3] Around this time he sold the name of the business, 'Purbeck Pottery', to a group of enterprising local businessmen, who then launched the Pottery that Purbeck is renowned for today. In this book we detail the story of this important company.

[1] John Aikin and William Johnston, *General Biography of Lives* (1815)

[2] *Design*, Issue 195 (published 1965)

[3] *Design*, Issue 211 (published 1966)

FOUNDING THE COMPANY AND INITIAL PRODUCTS

The name 'Purbeck Pottery' was purchased from Christopher Russell in 1966 but the concept of founding a new Dorset pottery was by then almost two years old. Several factors contributed to the idea of a new pottery venture. Firstly, the growing international trend for stoneware led by companies such as Denby and, secondly, the inability of Poole Pottery to meet this demand due to production capacity being stretched with both the 'Twintone' and 'Compact' ranges. Several of the employees at Poole recognised the obvious gap in the market but, in order to establish Purbeck, a stoneware body had to be developed.

To this end, Gordon Ede, the future 'Technical Director' of Purbeck, set to work in his garage with the aim of developing a once-fired stoneware body using ball clays mined only in the Purbeck Hills near Wareham in Dorset. After much experimentation, Ede "settled for a mixture of SM/TLD clays from Pike Fayle Ltd.".[1] This combination of clays was excellent for jolleying and throwing and, with the addition of fired grog, it could also be used for casting. The fact that the clay combination needed only one firing would lead to quick production of finished stoneware pieces, thereby giving the fledgling company an edge in the market. As the company literature proclaimed, "These clays are extremely fine and strong and, when fired to approximately 1260°C revert back to the non-porous, extremely strong stone from which they were originally formed many thousands of years ago".

Now Purbeck had a technical 'edge', but it also needed a design expert. Fortunately for Purbeck, Bob Jefferson, then resident designer at Poole Pottery, was ready to leave. In 1991, Jefferson memorably described his principal aim at Poole as "...not presenting the skills that were already there as a museum piece, but seeing where best they could be used in different ways".[2] By 1966, he had more than achieved this aim, steering Poole from Alfred Read's free-form image which Jefferson regarded as, "...so Festival of Britain and it wasn't 1951 any more...".[2]

The range of successful products which he had designed for Poole was quite incredible (more so when one considers that this was achieved in only eight years) but he had also designed so much that production was at full capacity. Jefferson had no more to do. As Peter Barnes succinctly explains, "Poole Pottery was really too small to have a resident designer and he was getting bored."[3]

Now that a talented designer was 'on board' and a new clay combination for producing once-fired stoneware was in place, new premises were needed. In the early months of 1966, Mr Stanley Laws (Managing Director of Purbeck Pottery) negotiated with Ernest Baggaley and eventually purchased the Branksome China premises in Seamoor Road, Westbourne, Bournemouth.

It was now decided that Purbeck Pottery should be established as a Limited Company, the founding Directors being Jack Turner (who provided financial backing and was appointed Chairman); Stanley Laws (Managing Director); Robert Jefferson (Design Director); Gordon Ede (Technical Director) and Peter Barnes (Sales Director).

With the exception of Jack Turner, all the other Directors had previously worked for Poole Pottery. Their departure angered Roy Holland (Managing Director at Poole) so much "...that his employees were forbidden to have anything to do with us or to sell us any equipment".[3] Peter Barnes was made to work out his three-months' notice at Poole, but paradoxically this suited the new venture perfectly. As Peter himself comments, "What was the use of having a Sales Director if there was nothing to sell?"[4]

The directors of the fledgling new Purbeck Pottery had a major task on their hands. The Westbourne premises (Illus 2) were dilapidated and needed completely renovating, a job which including the installation of a firegas openflare kiln. The existing kiln, made to Ernest Baggeley's design, "...required constant adjustments and attention"[3] and, as the kiln cycle needed for Purbeck's stoneware was ten to eleven hours, this clearly needed urgent replacement. When the new kiln was installed, it had a 150 cu. ft. capacity and could therefore accommodate two trucks. Cleverly, Gordon Ede with Jimmy Vaughan then added a turntable for cars to further increase the speed of production. Additional to the installation of a new kiln, floors had to be concreted and the building fully rewired.

Speed of production can make or break a new company, and the layout over the two floors was critical. As Gordon Ede indicates, "...much of the success must be attributed to our engineer, Jimmy Vaughan".[1]

The upper floor was used for manufacture, with hand-operated jolleys and moulds for casting jugs, teapots and coffee pots. The ground floor was used for glaze spraying, silkscreen

ILLUS 2 - *The Westbourne premises; Purbeck Pottery's first home*

13

printing, banding, firing and packing. This streamlining of the production process over two floors ensured that the space afforded by the new premises was used to full advantage. With a seconds shop in the block across the courtyard, the drive to production began in earnest.

As the venture was so new, employees had to assume multiple roles: "It's all hands on deck with a new enterprise, and nowhere can this be better demonstrated than in the slip-spraying department, where a sprayer is also a carpenter and builds racks to his own specification and convenience."[5]

All employees had to multitask and Peter Barnes was given the job of opening a china and glass shop in Seamoor Road, Westbourne, called 'The Purbeck Pedlar'.

Meanwhile, Bob Jefferson was busy with the talented designer and mould-maker, George Janes, producing the first of Purbeck's products. Many trials had to be undertaken with the new, highly vitrified, stoneware body and by September 1966 the first complete tableware range was being distributed in more than limited volume.

The 'Country Fare' range

The first full range of tableware to be designed was 'Country Fare'. Jefferson and Janes worked to develop an extensive range, which comprised:

i.   4 pint game pie casserole
ii.   2 pint casserole
iii.   Salt and pepper
iv.   Dinner plates
v.   Side plates
vi.   Cups and saucers
vii.   Teapot
viii. Milk jug
ix.   Sugar/preserve pot
x.   Oval platter

In design terms, the two casseroles were certainly the centrepiece of the range. Jefferson designed, and Janes made possible, the striking sculptural pheasant-shaped lids, beautifully rendered and unlike anything else available in stoneware. The two holes at the tail end were an essential design feature of the lidded casserole and, when sold, had two real pheasant feathers inserted - a wonderful marketing touch!

The range is unmistakeably Jefferson's, with the vertical fluting of his earlier 'Compact' range for Poole now a key feature of the 'Country Fare' hollowware, though it differs from 'Compact' in the way it softens and curves towards the base. This design element even extended into the lid of the teapot.

The 'Country Fare' range was produced in two patterns: 'Pheasant' and 'Oatmeal'.

'Pheasant' *(Illus 3)* used attractive stoneware glazes banded in greens and browns. This colourway proved extremely difficult to manufacture, as the coloured bands were hard to control. Consequently this was in production for only a few years. From a design perspective, 'Oatmeal' *(Illus 4)* was more successful. This was produced by spraying the outside of the wares with terracotta clay slip and then "…over spraying inside and out with a mixture of 1/3 transparent and 2/3 lime matt from EWT Mayer".[6]

The flatware has a 'Doily' pattern created by silk screening celadon colour onto paper, and then transferring to the Courlose-hardened-unfired-white-glaze mix. The slight celadon tinge is a feature of both the holloware and flatware, and the decoration works harmoniously with the design.

The 'Grecian' coffee set

The second major product was a coffee set with a Grecian 'feel' intended to be shaped more like porcelain than stoneware. This was clearly seen as separate from the 'Country Fare' range but, like 'Country Fare', Jefferson designed a striking centrepiece: the coffee pot *(Illus 5)*. The pot has a wide base tapering to a significantly narrower top. Combined with the elegant, wide, strap-like handle and elongated spout, the coffee pot certainly functioned as a defined design statement.

ILLUS 3 - *The 'Country Fare' range ('Pheasant' pattern)*
Original promotional photograph c.1967 ▼   **ILLUS 4** - *The 'Oatmeal'*
pattern tea set ▲   **ILLUS 5** - *The 'Grecian'*
▼ *coffee set 1967*   17

ILLUS 6 - *'Playing card' beakers*

Stylistically, one can see links with 'Contour' as the coffee pot feels like a 'stretched' version of the earlier Poole range. In a sense, this demonstrates Jefferson's organic approach to design; indeed gradual changes rather than radical shifts are a noted feature of many Purbeck Pottery products.

The 'Grecian' coffee set was marketed in a gold spot and gold-banded decoration over either matt black or matt brown glaze. In addition to the coffee pot and saucers the set came with 10oz beakers and 5oz cups. Both the cups and mugs used a striking combination of two different glaze bases – a gloss glaze on the inside and a matt on the exterior. This was labour intensive as the interior gloss glaze had to be manually poured in and out before the exterior was sprayed with the matt glaze.

Alternative Patterns for the Coffee Sets

In addition to the 'Country Fare' range and 'Grecian' coffee sets, Jefferson was also busy designing alternative patterns

for the 'Grecian' style mugs, the first of which were transfer-printed playing-card-inspired themes. The 'King and Queen' design was ready for production in March 1967. *(Illus 6)* This was rapidly followed with 'Medieval Scenes'. *(Illus 7)* The Medieval Scenes decoration reflects Jefferson's continuing interest in historical sources as an inspiration for patterns. Previously, at Poole, Jefferson had designed wall plaques with a low relief pattern based on a medieval illuminated manuscript page which prominently feature a castle as a dominant thematic motif.

At Purbeck, Jefferson returned to medieval iconography as a theme for the coffee mugs. The group, titled 'Medieval Pursuits' came in six different patterns:

i.   Hunting
ii. Hawking
iii. Jousting
iv. Feasting
v.   Crusaders
vi. Troubadours

ILLUS 8 - *'Greek Myths' beakers: Danae and the Shower of Gold*   **ILLUS 9** - *'Pop Art-inspired' beakers*

A further range, 'Greek Myths', was added shortly thereafter. *(Illus 8)*

Each of the mugs had gold decoration, which was popular in the 1960s and already employed by Staffordshire potteries such as Portmeirion.

In addition to these 'historical' patterns, the younger market needed to be catered for. A set of 'Pop Art inspired' mugs was, therefore produced. As Peter Barnes, head of 'The Purbeck Pedlar' shop, comments, "We stocked several well-known table and ovenware manufactures: Royal Worcester, Danish, Rosenthal, Minton – all fairly expensive. Westbourne, we decided, was populated by many affluent people who would find the tableware irresistible. However, although this was true, they had moved from big houses into flats in retirement. They had collected Minton or Worcester, had been given a set on retirement and wanted only to replace breakages and so wanted a cup and saucer. They were generous to their grandchildren and we built up a very good trade in modern tableware..."[3]

The 'Pop Art' pattern *(Illus 9)* had a lilac saucer with white-ground mugs over which are silk-screened psychedelic patterns of amoebic form and concentric circles bubbling across the surface. Today these represent a very rare find for the collector.

Further items produced in 1967 were the tankards, which were all handpainted with lustres and referred to as "something new in the way of stoneware decoration".[5]

Money Boxes

Jefferson's final early design (also in 1967) were three square money boxes in three sizes, "...intended for the head of the household, his wife and child respectively".[5] Initially these were printed in gold on black, and black on white, with stylistic representations of a bowler-hatted man; woman, and child. *(Illus 10)* A motto such as 'Save now pay later' and 'Do not open yet' was also included.

Later a transfer-printed 'Greek coin' motif in gold was added to the series and the 'Playing Card' theme was also incorporated as a third pattern.

The stylised 1960s iconography of the man, woman, and child set makes a particularly attractive collectable.

Jefferson had set a high design standard for the fledgling company and many leading department stores in the UK as well as in Australia (the first large order went to 'Georges' of Melbourne), South Africa, Canada, and New Zealand began to stock Purbeck. By February 1968, 75% of Purbeck's production was exported[7] but there were problems with both the 'Country Fare' range and the 'Grecian' coffee set. The 'Country Fare' range, despite the integrity of its design, was not the success that the company had hoped for. As Gordon Ede explains, "This range, unfortunately, did not excite the American market, which Stanley Laws was very keen to break into, so it was dropped."[1]

There were also problems with the packing of the delicate 'Grecian' coffee pot. Because it occupied a large volume of space, it required an even larger box, which was mainly empty, and therefore fewer could be dispatched per delivery thereby increasing costs.

Nevertheless, Purbeck had established a distinctive design presence in the marketplace. With further input from Bob Jefferson, a series of new products, which would take the company into the 1970s, would soon be developed.

[1] Letter to the authors from Gordon Ede (September 2007)

[2] Interview with Alan Peat (30th June 1991)

[3] Peter Barnes, *A brief history of Purbeck* (January 2000)

[4] Interview with authors (18th July 2007)

[5] Anonymous, 'Purbeck Pottery gets down to Production', *Pottery Gazette and Glass Trade Review* (March 1967)

[6] Letter to Alan Peat from Gordon Ede (October 2007)

[7] 'They Go Big Abroad', *Bournemouth Evening Echo* (26th February 1968)

CHAPTER 03 - 1967-69

BOB JEFFERSON'S CONTEMPORARY
SLIP-CAST STUDIO RANGE AND ORNAMENTS

BOB JEFFERSON'S CONTEMPORARY SLIP-CAST STUDIO RANGE & ORNAMENTS

The pinnacle of Jefferson's early work for Purbeck comes with the slip-cast vases, trays and ornaments designed between late 1967 and 1969. In early 1968 the *Bournemouth Evening Echo* described Purbeck's product range as "...dinner services, tea services, coffee sets and allied articles like ashtrays and bowls... everything manufactured is functional and not just decorative". [*1]

The fact that 'ashtrays and bowls' are mentioned allows us to date Jefferson's earliest 'fancies' – a series of small shallow circular dishes (5 inches in diameter) in three forms *(Illus 11)*.

The first of these is a personified sun motif; secondly a stylised snowflake motif (which may suggest a series based on the seasons though the authors have found no further patterns attributable to this series) and finally a stylised bird motif. All are slip-cast with raised low relief decoration which allows the glaze to pool in the recesses, thereby creating an attractive two-tone effect with one application of glaze – an economical way of creating a striking effect. All of the dishes can be found in two colourways, 'Oatmeal' and 'Blue-Green.' These colour choices suggest that they were designed to blend with the 'Country Fare' range.

ILLUS 11 - *Slip-cast shallow dishes with raised decoration. Robert Jefferson 1967/68*

Jefferson followed these small trays with a truly monumental range of fifteen 'studio-feel' vases and trays. *(Illus 12 & 13)* Of the fifteen pieces, eight are vases and seven are 'trays'. Although industrially produced, the range has a handbuilt look, something that Jefferson was keen to emphasise, going as far as designing a special backstamp, which could be impressed into the wares. *(Illus 14)* The hand and paintbrush motif allude to both art and handcrafting and also demonstrate Jefferson's minute attention to detail.

Having previously been Head of the design studio at Poole, Jefferson was keen to establish the studio-look aspect at Purbeck, and indeed the 'Slipcast Studio Range' was a great success.

Four of the vases are geometric in form with rough textured surfaces in matt brown shades with the biscuit exposed on the protruding low relief geometric forms. Mark Baker (who worked as a thrower for Purbeck in the 1980s and 90s) suggested that Jefferson was inspired by the work of Bernard Rooke. Rooke (along with Alan Wallwork) was certainly one of the most commercially successful of the early British handbuilders and Jefferson would undoubtedly have been familiar with his work.

26

ILLUS 12 - *Factory promotional photograph of* ▲
Jefferson's 'Slip-cast Studio' vases and trays

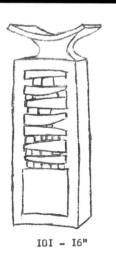

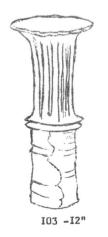

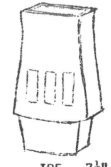

I00 - 16"   I0I - 16"   I02 - I0"   I03 -I2"   I04 - 7"   I05 - 7½"   I06 - 7"   I07 - 8

ILLUS 13 - *Purbeck pattern book illustrations with factory production numbers* ▼

▲ **ILLUS 14** - *Backstamp for the 'Slip-cast Studio Range'*

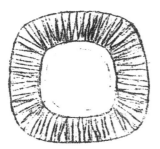

I08A - 7"

I08B - 7"

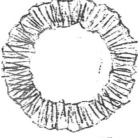

I09 - 7"

II0 - 6"

IIIA - 4"

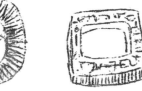

IIIB - 4"

TT2 - 8"

Whether or not Rooke's work was the specific 'trigger' for Jefferson's designs is debatable but they would have appeared daringly contemporary in 1969. As Paul Rice stated, "...it is almost impossible to realize how much handbuilding was a totally revolutionary concept in British studio ceramics before the late 1950s". [2]

Less than ten years later, after the handbuilding of pottery began in England, Jefferson was successfully creating the same handbuilt-look in an industrial setting. The simple geometrics and wide flaring lips make these vases particularly attractive to a collector. All have glazed interiors and are therefore capable of holding water, making them both beautiful and functional, a hallmark of Jefferson's work.

The remaining four vases are more biomorphic in form with the 'Tulip Head' (Pattern 106) being particularly rare, as it was not made in large numbers. One of the vases (Pattern 107) is of a pot-bellied form and when all are considered as a whole one can see that Jefferson was designing for wide-market appeal.

The same is true of the small trays. Patterns 108B and 111B can be viewed as a development of the small shallow circular 'sun motif' dishes of 1968. Both have a central sun motif but instead of the delicate modelling of the earlier dishes these are heavily cast with a textural bark-patterning around the circumference.

The other trays use melted glass in the central hollow. Crushed glass bottles were used and, to create the vivid jewel-like colours, cobalt was added to create a translucent blue and copper for green. The brown-yellow colour was simply obtained by using brown-coloured bottles. (Purple variants are also found, though these are less common.)

Interestingly one of the designs, pattern 112 *(Illus 15)*, has a stylised rune-like alphabet applied as a border. This lends more credence to the idea that Jefferson was influenced by the work of studio potter Bernard Rooke, as both Rooke and Alan Wallwork used invented rune-like alphabets as a decorative device.

ILLUS 15 - *Rune-bordered shallow trays from the 'Slip-cast Studio Range'*

The range is, however, far from derivative and Jefferson's real achievement is the successful crossover between studio and industrially produced pottery.

Additionally during this period at Purbeck Pottery, Jefferson produced a circular glazed slip-cast ashtray with a raised stylised sun motif at its centre. *(Illus 16)* The brown and yellow 'soap bubble' glaze was also used to decorate shallow-footed bowls. A further decorative approach used by Jefferson was wax resist – trays with patterns of blue and yellow glaze on a black ground (giving a stained-glass-window effect) have been found by the authors.

It is interesting to note that these were not the only slip-cast decorative pieces which Jefferson produced for the company. He also made a slip-cast female figurine, commissioned by a hotel in Bournemouth for use in its bathrooms. Philip Barnes reused the mould to cast a small number for the Millennium in 2000, and Mark Baker recently produced a further six. These later castings are clearly identifiable as they mention Jefferson on the backstamp.

Jefferson realised that many customers would prefer naturalistic designs and so, after the initial figurine commission, he quickly turned his hand to the more traditional 'Wildlife Series' explored in the next chapter. This form of modelling would become increasingly important in the many commissions for Royal Doulton and Crown Derby, which he received after leaving Purbeck.

ILLUS 16 - *Large slip-cast ashtray, Robert Jefferson* ▶

*1 'Industrial Survey', *Bournemouth Evening Echo* (26th February 1968)

*2 Paul Rice, *British Studio Ceramics* (Crowood Press, 2002)

31

JEFFERSON'S TRADITIONAL 'WILDLIFE' SERIES

In the early 1970s Purbeck Pottery was approached by the leading independent Dorset brewer, Hall and Woodhouse to create a model to advertise their 'Badger Beer' brand. The popular 'Wildlife' series stemmed from this initial commission and demonstrates Jefferson's skill as a naturalistic modeller.

The first series consisted of twelve items all of which were modelled by Jefferson:

i.   Otter

ii.   Gerbil

iii.   Squirrel

iv.   Hare

v.   Dartmoor Pony

vi.   Badger

vii.   Hedgehog (adult)

viii.   Hedgehog (baby)

ix.   Owl

x.   Fox cub (sitting upright)

xi.   Fox cub (sitting down)

xii.   Adult fox

After Jefferson's departure in the mid-1970s the series was modified. Both the 'Adult Fox' and 'Dartmoor Pony' ceased production. The Dartmoor Pony was the most difficult to produce and fewer than 500 were made, making this animal the rarest in the series. The deleted 'Adult Fox' is also a particularly rare find.

Three new animals were, however, added to the modified series:

i.   Badger (baby)

ii.   Owl (baby)

iii.   Frog (*Illus 17*)

The modeller for the additional three items was Bruce Sydenham who also had the skilled task of decorating the animals. Super 8 footage remains of Sydenham using an airbrush to paint the creatures. The complexity of the task is obvious as Sydenham rotates the model rather than the airbrush.

Sydenham retired in the late 1980s but before ending at Purbeck he trained a young man to decorate the animals. He stayed for about two years, leaving shortly after Bruce Sydenham's retirement, thereby ending formal production at Purbeck.

Upon retirement, Bruce Sydenham, did, however, take some moulds with him and so later versions, some with adapted plinths can be found. A 'BS' monogram scratched into the base identifies these items. Some pieces made during his employment are marked with both 'Purbeck' and his monogram.

Wild Life Series
by PURBECK

Although this series showed none of the daring of Jefferson's slip-cast studio range, it does demonstrate his flexibility, a necessary survival skill when working for a small industrial pottery such as Purbeck. Jefferson would no doubt have been aware that items such as those he designed for the 'Wildlife' series were popular sellers for firms such as Wade, Hornsea and Beswick. They certainly were a valuable addition to Purbeck's broadening range of products.

JEFFERSON'S FURTHER RANGES

The 'Plymouth' Range (1968)

The next major tableware range which Jefferson designed is 'Plymouth', a 22-item range initially released (late 1968) in five colourways (*Illus 18 & 19*):

i.   Honeydale

ii.   Greenvale

iii.   Dover

iv.   Sierra

v.   Toast

The flatware was retained from the 'Country Fare' range. Indeed, all ranges from this point evidence the company's evolutionary approach to design. But Purbeck certainly wasn't resting on its design laurels, as many new elements were designed into the 'Plymouth' range. (*Illus 20*)

The company literature stressed that the new range was "very tough, highly resistant to chipping. Completely vitrified and impervious to liquids, dishwasher safe".

Interestingly Purbeck's sales material also emphasised stackability and 'versatility': "...soup bowls can be used in the oven to cook and serve individual recipes".

This approach to marketing was taken, in the mid-1960s, by several other successful pottery companies (such as W.R. Midwinter), though stackability was, of course, a feature of Jefferson's earlier 'Compact' range (1965) for Poole.

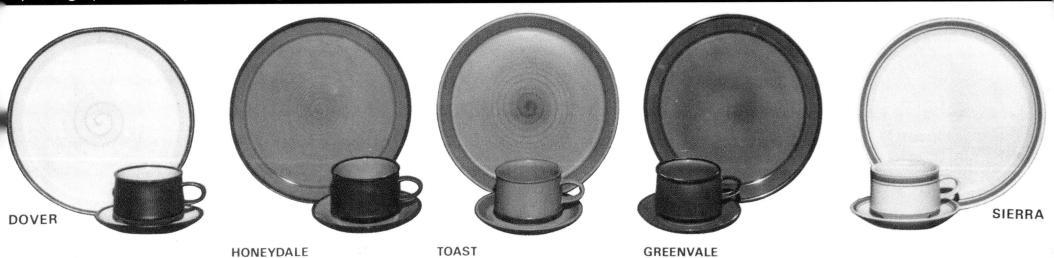

DOVER

HONEYDALE

TOAST

GREENVALE

SIERRA

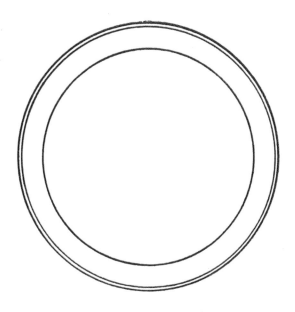

Plate 10, 8½, 7 inch
Teller flach 25, 21, 18 cm
assiette plate 25, 21, 18 cm

Chop Dish 12 inch
Platte rund 30 cm
plat rond 30 cm

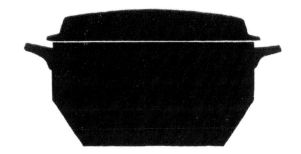

Casserole 4 pint
Kasserolle rund 2,00 liter
casserole ronde 2,00 litres

Fruit/Salad Server 8 inch/2½ pint
Salatschale rund 20 cm/1,25 liter
saladier rond 20 cm/1,25 litres

Teapot 2¼ pint
Teekanne 1,20 liter
théière 1,20 litres

Salt and Pepper
Salz & Pfeffer
Sel & Poivre

Onion Soup 12 oz
Butterpfännchen 0,35 liter
caquelon à beurre 0,35 litres

Sauce boat ½ pint
Saucière 0,25 liter/litres

Stand 6 inch
Untersatz 15 cm
Dessous 15 cm

Preserve 12 oz
Honigdose 0,35 liter
confiturier 0,35 litres

Jug 1 pint : 10 oz : 8 oz
Milchgiesser 0,5 : 0,35 : 0,25 te
pot à lait 0,5 : 0,35 : 0,25 litre

Lugged Soup 12 oz
Suppentasse 0,35 liter 11,5 cm
tasse à consommé 0,35 litres 11,5 cm

Coffee Pot 3 pint
Kaffeekanne 1,50 liter
cafetière 1,50 litres

Cup 8 oz
Tasse 0,25 liter/litres

Saucer 6 inch
Untertasse 15 cm
soustasse 15 cm

Eggcup
Eierbecher
Coquetier

Mug 12 oz
Becher m/Hkl. 0,35 liter
gobelet à anse 0,35 litres

Soup/Cereal 12 oz
Suppenbol 0,35 liter 11,5 cm
bol à potage 0,35 litres 11,5 cm

Oval Baker 12 inch
Backplatte oval 30 cm
plat ovale à gratin 30 cm

Fruit Nappie 7 oz
Schälchen rund 0,20 liter 11,5 cm
bol rond 0,20 litres 11,5 cm

Soup Stand 6 inch
Untertasse 15 cm
soustasse 15 cm

Covered Sugar 8 oz
Zuckerdose m/D. 0,25 liter
sucrier avec couvercle 0,25 litres

Open Sugar 8 oz
Zuckerschale 0,25 liter 9 cm
bol à sucre 0,25 litres 9 cm

Purbeck Pottery Ltd., Seamoor Road, Bournemouth, BH4 9AQ, England

One of the major differences between the earlier 'Country Fare' range and 'Plymouth' relates to the coffeeware. When 'Country Fare' was released, the 'Grecian' coffee pot and accompanying mugs and cups were an entirely separate design entity; with 'Plymouth' they are an integral part of the tableware range. Indeed, the design of the elongated, horizontal handles of the earlier 'Grecian' mugs has been transferred onto the cups, mugs and jugs of the 'Plymouth' range. This unity was undeniably demonstrated when the range was first photographed for *Pottery Gazette and Glass Trade Review* (May 1968) and the 'Plymouth' coffee set was not shown separately. It could, however, still be purchased as a 'stand-alone' set with a gold-banded decoration *(Illus 23)*. In a sense this demonstrates the rapid progress being made by Purbeck within a very short period of time. Within twelve months, the design direction was more unified than previously; there was far greater stylistic harmony.

Of particular importance in relation to Jefferson's approach to design is the 'Plymouth' gravy/sauce boat. *(Illus 21)* It retains the single 'lug/side bar' used in the 'Country Fare' range (interestingly, the origins of this 'lug' can be found in the work of the studio potter Lucie Rie, once again demonstrating the impact of studio pottery on Jefferson's work in an industrial context) but now instead of one pouring lip there are two, set opposite each other. This represents a significant ergonomic improvement on the 'Country Fare' range as gravy/sauce could now be poured with equal ease by both left-handed and right-handed people. The double pourer demonstrates that Jefferson would not sacrifice functionality at the 'altar of fashion'. His particular talent was one of seamlessly merging practicality with contemporary styling.

Although the mugs originally designed for the 'Grecian' coffee set were retained, the coffee pot and teapot were entirely new. The coffee pot is basically a long thin cylinder with an inward sloping, truncated base. The spout is also truncated, and in silhouette one can see how the angle of the downward –pointing strap handle follows though into the angle of the truncated spout. Seemingly minor design elements as this demonstrate Jefferson's meticulous attention to detail which is only matched in Susan William Ellis' popular 'Totem' range (1963) for Portmeirion. The result is a design which was very 'of the moment'. W.R. Midwinter had attempted a similar design in their 'Portobello' range (1966) *(Illus 22)* designed by Canadian craft potter David Long. Although this range is interesting, and also includes the elongated-bodied coffee pot with truncated spout, Long was only briefly 'bought into' W.R. Midwinter Ltd whereas Jefferson was an integral part of Purbeck.

▲ **ILLUS 22** - *W.R. Midwinter Ltd 'Portobello' range*

45

ILLUS 23 - 'Plymouth' 'stand-alone'
coffee and tea set with gold banding

The use of wood as a fundamental part of the range was daring stylistically but also, as you would expect, totally explicable in practical terms. From a design perspective it is another example of a studio pottery crossover. From a practical point of view the use of a wooden lid on the coffee pot and covered sugar bowl is sensible as these lids are removed most often in usage. There is a far greater risk of damage when a ceramic lid is placed on a ceramic pot than when a wooden lid is used.

It is also a further example of how Jefferson's designs gradually improved over time. In his 1965 'Compact' range for Poole, Jefferson had created a flat ceramic lid but this led to the problem of overheating. The lid became overly hot and was difficult to remove by customers. At Poole the problem was resolved by Tony Morris who, in 1969, remodelled the lids of the 'Compact' range by adding a knob to the lid. Clearly Jefferson did not like the design compromise and so retained the design integrity of the preferred flat lid by changing the material it was made of. Once more the end result is one of perfectly balanced form and functionality.

The teapot, which has an oriental-feel, also employs the use of wood for its handle which is made from a single piece of bent bamboo.

There are other stylistic cues which unify the range, the most obvious being the soft-ribbed, truncated bases on all the hollowware items.

The most successful colourways utilise a contrast between interior and exterior colour, a more overt way of adding variety than the use of gloss interior/matt exterior combinations on the 'Grecian' mugs. The company evidently recognised this and chose 'Dover' (which has the greater colour contrast) as the main design for the sales literature.

As Peter Barnes commented, "His second range was very successful, and because transfer manufacturers required large quantity runs, he relied on brushwork or embossments in the clay for decoration." [1]

From a collector's perspective the two rarest colourways are 'Greenvale" and 'Sierra' which ceased production as early as August 1972; 'Greenvale' because the colourway did not sell, and 'Sierra' which also did not sell well despite being selected by the London Design Centre. Another uncommon colourway is the original 'Toast' decoration for 'Plymouth'. Initially the outer glaze produced a cork-like textural effect. As Peter Barnes describes it, "The original 'Toast', in my opinion, was marvellous but varied, and the works wanted something a bit more controllable." [2] Sadly, this meant that the original 'cork' effect was reduced to a much 'flatter' orange colour with the brown banding.

'Plymouth' did not replace 'Country Fare' but ran alongside it. As Peter Barnes states, "That was one of the things we felt we had to do...we wanted to say to someone that in ten years' time, if you wanted to, you could come round and replace a piece." [2]

Diamond Range (1971)

Jefferson was designing continuously and the next range to evolve from 'Plymouth' was 'Diamond'. The hollowware remained the same as 'Plymouth' but the flatware was totally redesigned. Plates now had a diamond-patterned condiment rim, yet another example of the blending of design and function. The condiment rim obviously gave diners somewhere to place their condiments whilst also providing a new surface for decoration. The decorative element now enhances the food rather than being hidden, as was the case in the 'Country Fare' and 'Plymouth' ranges. It is interesting to note that the decorative surface of 'Country Fare' was vulnerable to scratching during use, whereas the patterned element of the 'Diamond' range is an integral aspect rather than an applied element of the design. The diamond pattern itself was impressed into the surface so that, once jolleyed, it merely needed painting and towing so that only the colour remained in the recesses.

This move away from two-stage decoration (matt interior/banded gloss interior) also further sped production, necessary in an increasingly competitive marketplace.

Although there were four colourways, the 'Diamond' range was originally released with only three, *(Illus 24)*

i.   Brown Diamond
ii. Blue Diamond
iii. Black Diamond

ILLUS 24 - *'Diamond' range in original three colourways* 47

'Blue Diamond' and 'Black Diamond' proved to be the least popular with the workforce producing them. Cobalt was needed to produce 'Blue Diamond' and, as Philip Barnes commented, "It flashed all over the place." [2] Peter Barnes adds that "Cobalt gets everywhere" with a final comment that "Everything you touched got blue on it." As a result, less of this ware was produced than other colourways making it something of a rarity. It also proved to be an unpopular colour with consumers.

ILLUS 25 - *Factory promotional leaflet for 'Portland"*

As Peter Barnes comments, "At the time there were lots of greens on the market. Denby had green and we thought, it's got to change; this year it's got to be blue. It never was!" [*2]

'Black Diamond' was equally unpopular at the factory because of the inconsistent results achieved. 'Black Diamond' has an all-over colour rather than just colour added to the perimeter and it proved "...the most difficult to control. Black was an exceedingly difficult colour. If you placed it in a certain part of the kiln it came out very bright.". [*2] Philip Barnes added that "...some areas shone, some areas had a silver shine to them.".[*2] The effect they were hoping to achieve was a "...silver fox effect, flecks of silver in the black". [*2] These perfect examples are elusive and are prized by a collector.

The final colourway, 'Buttermilk', came about for pragmatic reasons. Manganese was in short supply in the late 1970s and so a speckled white glaze was applied instead. Often referred to as 'Buttermilk', this glaze was later adapted to the 'Rondo' range as 'Dover Rondo'.

Post –'Diamond' Ranges

Jefferson's final tableware ranges for Purbeck, 'Portland' and 'Studland' were released simultaneously circa 1973.

1. PORTLAND (Reduced ware)

The Portland shape (Illus 25) had been under development for some time. Philip Barnes noted, " He played around with Portland from the beginning. I remember seeing Portland in his little kiln down at Upton." [2] 'Portland' utilises the same tapering-footed base as the holloware of the 'Plymouth' and the 'Diamond' ranges but has additional incised, concentric bands that form a design feature directly above the footed base. The banding on the mug works particularly well as it emphasises its height, though sadly the application of a new handle to the coffee pot results in the loss of the 'through line' between handle and spout. The dominance of the concentric banding is further accentuated by the newly designed tapering lugs on the soup dish and casserole. This replaced the flat, square-like handles of the previous ranges, and provides a continuity of design-aesthetic to the range.

The flatware has an inward tapering rim that runs into the base of the plate with no defined edge. Again the rim is decorated by the banded motif.

This range with the classic grey speckle and iron-oxide-reduced edging is still sold today, a longevity unusual in the fickle ceramics market.

Later the popular pattern 'Toast' was applied to the 'Portland' shape but the 'Diamond' range cup was retained instead of the new high-banded one.

2. STUDLAND

'Studland' (Illus 26 & 27) was released simultaneously with 'Portland". The major difference between 'Studland' and 'Portland' lies in the flatware. The plate has concentric grooves cut into the condiment rim, a new stylistic feature.

Plate 10 ins
Plate 8½ ins.
Plate 7 ins.
Chop dish 12 ins.

Oval steak plate 12 ins.
Oval steak plate 10¼ ins.

Butter pat

Egg cup 1½ ins.
Mustard 2½ ins.

Salt/pepper 3 ins.
Salt/pepper 5 ins.
Salt/pepper 3 ins.

Soup/cereal/bowl lid

Pie dish/vegetable dish lid

Fruit dish/ice cream

Large soup 20 oz.
Soup/cereal 15 oz.

Vegetable/salad dish 3 pint.

Spaghetti/salad bowl

Lugged soup 15 oz.

Sauce Boat 1 pint

TRADITIONAL SHAPE

Mug ½ pint
Beaker 7oz.

CONICAL SHAPE

Butter dish lid

Oval butter dish

Goblet 6 oz.

Mug ½ pint
Beaker 7 oz

Mug ½ pint
Beaker 7 oz
Cup 9 oz.
Cup 7 oz.

ILLUS 26 - *Factory silhouettes for Studland, Dover, Toast and Portland*   49

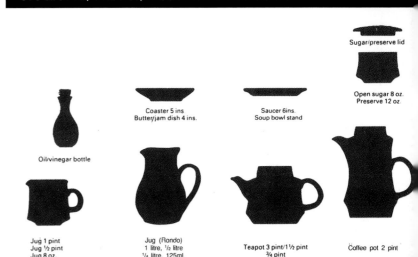

Sugar/preserve lid

Open sugar 8 oz.
Preserve 12 oz.

Oil/vinegar bottle

Coaster 5 ins
Butter/jam dish 4 ins.

Saucer 6ins.
Soup bowl stand

Jug 1 pint
Jug ½ pint
Jug 8 oz.

Jug (Rondo)
1 litre, ½ litre
¼ litre, 125ml.

Teapot 3 pint/1½ pint
¾ pint

Coffee pot 2 pint

'Studland' flatware is identical in shape to the 'Diamond', range but with the altered decorative feature of concentric banded grooves to the condiment rim. Studland has the distinctive olive-green colour not found on 'Plymouth'. Later 'Studland' was released in a plain speckled white colourway called 'Dover' which, like 'Studland', is still available from the company.

Jefferson continued to experiment but, as at Poole, he had designed so much that there were problems. As Peter Barnes states in an undated letter written some time later, "...unfortunately our production was fully involved with little likelihood of being able to introduce any new designs and, although Robert was interested in producing enamels and some jewellery, it was not economic for the pottery to employ him and, unfortunately, we parted company."

In the ranges still currently available we see the longevity of Jefferson's designs. His impact on the company had been tremendous and it is a legacy, which Purbeck pottery acknowledges to this day.

[1] Undated Letter from Peter Barnes

[2] Interview with Peter & Philip Barnes (18th July 2007)

Studland   Dover   Toast   Portland

THROWN DECORATIVE WARES

In 1971, Eddie Goodall replaced Bill Jones as resident thrower at Purbeck. A decision was made to extend Purbeck's range in order to include a broader range of thrown items and Eddie Goodall (and later Mark Baker) and for a short time Russel Sydenham (Guy Sydenham's son) filled this role.

Eddie had learned the basics of pottery whilst at school and was initially appointed as a slip-sprayer at Poole Pottery in 1959. He had wanted to be a painter but unfortunately in the late 1950s only females were employed in that capacity at Poole. The slip-spraying shop was directly opposite the throwing shop and Goodall would often watch Guy Sydenham (head thrower at Poole) during his breaks. As a result of his interest Sydenham allowed him to throw pots during his lunch hour.

Dissatisfied with slip-spraying, Goodall requested that he should be apprenticed under Sydenham. Initially Sydenham was reluctant, as the apprenticeship was of seven years' duration and the previous incumbent had left part-way through his term. Eventually the Managing Director at Poole, Roy Holland, made the decision to apprentice Goodall to Sydenham.

Goodall was clearly a talented thrower, as can be seen in this early piece *(Illus 28)* made while still under apprenticeship to Sydenham. Interestingly the incising and 'hacksaw-blade cut' vertical lines were to become a feature of some of his early work at Purbeck.

Goodall started immediately as a thrower at Purbeck in 1971 but was initially daunted by the prospect of designing whilst a designer of Jefferson's reputation was still at the factory. He had no need to worry as his pots actually extended the company's product line.

The earliest of Goodall's work are a rare find for collectors, but are easily recognised as they have several definable features:

i.   Eddie Goodall's monogram. (See Appendix, page 70.) Later pieces were not impressed with the monogram owing to the increased need for fast production.

ii.   Roughly incised decoration – sun motifs and concentric circles were particularly popular.

iii. A dark brown exterior rubbed or scraped through to reveal the lighter brown underneath.

Some of his early vases also employed the hacksaw-scratched banding.

If one considers Jefferson's work, one can see that the new vases[1] were designed to harmonise with Jefferson's designs. This is effectively demonstrated in the hand-thrown bowl here seen in *Illus 29*. The bowl has Goodall's clearly impressed monogram at its base but also employs the central crazed-glass decoration first used on Jefferson's 'Slipcast Studio' range (see page 24). The incised sun motif pots may, therefore, also have been designed to harmonise with Jefferson's personified 'sun face' ashtrays, also from the 'Slipcast Studio' range.

ILLUS 28 - *Early apprentice piece by Eddie Goodall*

ILLUS 29 - *Bowl combining Jefferson's 'Slip-cast Studio' crazed glaze decoration with Goodall's 'hacksaw-blade' texturing*

55

*¹ There is much debate among the remaining ex-Purbeck workers as to who deserves credit for many of the thrown wares of this period, with some crediting Goodall, others Jefferson and others George Janes, the mould maker. The authors wish to acknowledge the range of opinions regarding this matter.

ILLUS 30 - *Early pin dish and rimmed trays (Eddie Goodall)*

Several of the hand-thrown pots also have a distinctive inward tapering base, already a feature of the hollowware items from the 1968 'Plymouth' range.

Goodall also threw 3 ½ inch pin dishes with a glass centre together with 5, 6 and 8 ½ inch rimmed trays *(Illus 30)*. The earlier ones (with the monogram) are particularly rare and they were quickly replaced by slip-cast versions, which are not monogrammed. The end of monogrammed work coincides with Jefferson's departure in 1974. With a drive towards increased production, it was one fewer process to employ. Other changes also occurred at this time, including the redesign of the Jefferson 'back-to-back double P' backstamp,

which was altered to a more modern font. (Appendix, page 71)

At a similar time Jefferson's final pieces for Purbeck were produced. These all employed incised rather than raised decoration. One range of footed bowls all employed incised

naturalistic decoration, which includes:

i.   Blue tits *(Illus 31)*

ii.   Angelfish

iii.   Owl facing right

iv.   Jay

v.   Eagle (with RJ monogram)

These all employ the same colour combination as 'Blue Diamond'. In addition to the naturalistic bowls, there was also an abstract floral spray *(Illus 31)*, and a 'Four Nations' bowl which included naturalistic symbols for England, Ireland, Scotland and Wales.

Commemorative-ware items, which relate to specific locations, were also produced e.g Liverpool, Albert Square,

Manchester, Poole Customs House etc. Small shallow circular dishes with incised semi-abstract (dove and olive branch) and abstract geometric decorations also exist. *(Illus 32)*

The earlier 'rubbed through' dark brown vases *(Illus 33)* were then replaced with 24 different shapes. These included bud vases, standard vases and lamp bases. The earlier incising disappears and instead a range of new decorative features occurs.

59

ILLUS 34 - *Multicoloured, Sheila Drew painted group (4 initialled, 1 unsigned)*

ILLUS 35 - *Knurled borders with hand textured centres*

Some of Goodall's hand-thrown pots were handpainted by talented painter Sheila Drew who was employed on a part-time basis from 1973. Her work is predominately floral and is found in either single or multiple colours. Some, though not all, are initialled in paint within the design. Her decorations are mainly found on vases, lamp bases, plates and footed bowls (*Illus 34*). The standard is high, as Purbeck never in-troduced 'piece work' (as was the case at Poole at this time).

The second distinctive decorative technique, which is a feature of many Purbeck pieces, is the use of knurled bands enclosing a textural centre. The knurling was achieved by placing a handmade toothed wooden cogwheel, with teeth of differing sizes for different patterns, in a pastry wheel.

ILLUS 36 - *Decorative bowls in 'Brown Diamond' colourway;
some with glass centres*

The more elaborate central applied slip band, between the knurled borders, was hand-textured by George Janes prior to firing, in order to lend a rough 'studio' appeal. *(Illus 35-36)*

The range was clearly popular as Goodall was joined by Mark Baker, who made all the hand-thrown pieces after Eddie's departure from Purbeck in 1989. Mark was introduced to Purbeck on a 'work experience' placement in 1978 and was appointed after two weeks. His initial apprenticeship was in all aspects of the company's production but he excelled at throwing and between 1989 and 1991 was the sole thrower at Purbeck. His final job for the company, in 1991, was the production of vases for the liner *Canberra*.

THE 'RONDO' AND 'ZDENKA' RANGES

THE 'RONDO' AND 'ZDENKA' RANGES

In 1992 the two remaining original directors, Gordon Ede and Peter Barnes, retired, handing over responsibility for Purbeck to their sons, Philip and Simon Barnes and Darrell and Varden Ede, who had different visions as to how the company might develop and as a result a demerger occurred in January 1993. As a consequence of this demerger, Philip and Simon retained sole company directorship.

In light of such changes it is remarkable that a new range, 'Rondo' *(Illus 37),* was designed by George Janes and Philip Barnes in 1993. 'Rondo' retained the flatware of 'Portland' but with newly designed cups and jugs.

The hollowware loses all angularity and has soft flowing lines.

The cups are also rounded and shallower than previous designs, and the teapot effectively mirrors the lines of the jug.

'Rondo' was released in the same colourways as Portland, Studland, Dover and Toast and also with a new transfer-printed naturalistic strawberry pattern.

Further changes occurred rapidly, the most significant of which was the move from Westbourne to Hamworthy, Poole in 1996. This necessitated a change to the backstamp with the word 'Poole' replacing 'Bournemouth.' To mark this new phase in the company's development, Zdenka Ralph was commissioned to design a further range.

Released in 1996, the 'Zdenka' range *(Illus 38)* is basically 'Rondo' but with the addition of conical salt and pepper pots. These relate stylistically to Clarice Cliff's 'Bizarre' ware, so popular with Art Deco ceramic collectors.

Ralph's work makes an attractive addition to any Purbeck collection. As she had previously worked for Poole Pottery, the three patterns she designed have a distinctive appeal. 'Ivy' *(Illus 39)* is a sponged decoration; 'Grapevine' is a bold handpainted design and 'Chicken' combines handpainting and sponging. Additionally double-handled amphora-type pots were produced in a 'Sea horse' pattern and a 'Leaf Motif' (which coordinates well with the 'Chicken' range).

In a market dominated by bland transfer-printed designs, Purbeck created three individual, strong new patterns. The range, sadly, is no longer being produced (the handpainting made this a particularly expensive purchase) but this is by no means the end of Purbeck.

ILLUS 37 - *The 'Rondo' range*

ILLUS 38 - *The 'Zdenka' range in 'Grapevine' pattern*

ILLUS 39 - *The 'Zdenka' range in 'Ivy' pattern*

The market that pottery producers find themselves in today is an increasingly competitive one but, with a design tradition of over thirty years, Purbeck Pottery is strongly placed for retaining its edge in the marketplace. The company was streamlined in 2006 when the Hamworthy plant closed and currently production rests with Mark Baker, the talented thrower who trained under Eddie Goodall at Purbeck.

Mark produces his own pots at 'The Courtyard Centre' at Lytchett Minister near Poole and is currently working with Philip Barnes on a new studio range. The early trial pieces have a clear Purbeck 'feel' and individuality. The British pottery industry certainly needs such individuality, and Purbeck's latest creations are a far cry from the blandness of much of the commercial pottery currently being produced. We hope that they will long continue to produce such pottery.

BACKSTAMPS

BACKSTAMP 1
1966-1974
General printed mark used on tableware and decorative wares

BACKSTAMP 2
1967-1968
Impressed mark found on early 'Country Fare' flatware

BACKSTAMP 3
1968-1974
Small label, found on the unglazed 'Plymouth' teapot bases and early carafe sets

BACK STAMP 4
1967-
Printed in gold. Used on the 'Greek Myths' range, coffee cans

BACKSTAMP 5
1967-
Impressed mark found on the 'Slip-cast Studio' range flatware

BACKSTAMP 6
1971-1974
Impressed mark, the monogram of Eddie Goodall

Purbeck Pottery
Vitrified
English Stoneware
Made from the
Dorset Purbeck Clays
Fully resistant to Oven shock
Designed by Robert Jefferson Des. RCA

Purbeck
Pottery England
GREEK MYTHS
Danae and the Shower of Gold

BACKSTAMP 7
1974-1976
Transition period label (larger than 'Backstamp 3'), found on decorative ware such as the engraved animal series and early bud vases

BACKSTAMP 8
1976-1996
'New' logo transfer used on decorative plates. Variants include 'Purbeck Pottery' linearly written and the addition of 'English stoneware. Made from clays mined from the Purbeck hills near Corfe Castle.'

BACKSTAMP 9
1976-1992
Large label, used on decorative ware and hand-thrown vases

BACKSTAMP 10
1976(?)-1992(?)
Large label, less common variation of Label 3

BACKSTAMP 11
1972-1990(?)
Scratched into the base of the 'wildlife' series. May also include the animal type, and wording 'Wildlife series, Purbeck, England.'

BACKSTAMP 12
1996-2006
Hamworthy period

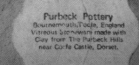

Same as **Backstamp 8** but with 'Poole' replacing 'Bournemouth'

DATING

Dating Purbeck pieces can be a potentially difficult affair, due to the long production runs of some of the ranges. However, with the use of backstamps and stylistic features, approximate dating can be achieved.

The first backstamp, that of the back-to-back P's, was designed by Jefferson at the start of the company's history in 1966 and is included on all the ware from then until Jefferson's departure in 1974. The flatware of the 'Country Fare' range initially had a more elaborate impressed mark, 'Backstamp 2', but later reverted to 'Backstamp 1'.

For the next range, 'Plymouth', Jefferson designed a different backstamp, which consisted of the standard logo and the addition of the words 'Plymouth Stoneware'. However this was not uniformly adopted and pieces will be found with 'Backstamp 1'.

'Backstamp 3' appears to have been used on the slip-cast teapots, and the large platters for the early carafes. These labels were introduced because the aforementioned pieces had no footed rim. They sat directly on their base and so a painted backstamp was impossible as it would smudge in the firing.

Later tableware (post-1974) dispensed with backstamping, so identification using 'range knowledge' is crucial. Subtle stylistic design changes occurred in some of the earlier ranges. These also give the collector dating evidence. One main area of change was the cup and beaker handles. Jefferson's original design had elongated horizontal handles (used on the 'Plymouth' and 'Diamond'). In the early 1980s they were replaced with a chunkier, more conventional rounded handle.

Jefferson's departure in mid-1974 was soon followed by the untimely death of another founding director, Stanley Laws. This led to a restructuring of the company with Gordon Ede taking over as Managing Director, and Peter Barnes as Commercial Manager. With these changes came a redesign of the company logo and by 1976 the new 'space-age' logo was being used in company-promoted materials etc. This coincided with the introduction of a simpler paper label for hand-thrown and decorative wares.

The final change to the backstamps occurred after the company's move to Hamworthy in 1996. 'Backstamp 8' was modified to simply read 'Purbeck Pottery Poole, England'.

Goblet 6 oz.

Mug ½ pint
Beaker 7 oz

Mug ½ pint
Beaker 7 oz
Cup 9 oz.
Cup 7 oz.

Coaster 5 ins.
Butter/jam dish 4 ins.

Saucer 6ins.
Soup bowl stand

Lugged Soup 12 oz
Suppentasse 0,35 liter 11,5 cm
tasse à consommé 0,35 litres 11,5 cm

Oil/vinegar bottle

Plate 10, 8½, 7 inch
Teller flach 25, 21, 18 cm
assiette plate 25, 21, 18 cm

Casserole 4 pint
Kasserolle rund 2,00 liter
casserole ronde 2,00 litres

Fruit/Salad Server 8 inch/2¼ pint
Salatschale rund 20 cm/1,25 liter
saladier rond 20 cm/1,25 litres

Teapot 2¼ pint
Teekanne 1,20 liter
théière 1,20 litres

Coffee Pot 3 pint
Kaffeekanne 1,50 liter
cafetière 1,50 litres

Cup 8 oz
Tasse 0,25 liter/litres

Eggcup
Eierbecher
Coquetier

Mug 12 oz
Becher m/Hkl. 0,35 liter
gobelet à anse 0,35 litres

Soup/Cereal 12 oz
Suppenbol 0,35 liter 11,5 cm
bol à potage 0,35 litres 11,5 cm

Chop Dish 12 inch
Platte rund 30 cm
plat rond 30 cm

Oval butter dish

Saucer 6 inch
Untertasse 15 cm
soustasse 15 cm

Salt and Pepper
Salz & Pfeffer
Sel & Poivre

Onion Soup 12 oz
Butterpfännchen 0,35 liter
caquelon à beurre 0,35 litres

Sauce boat ½ pint
Saucière 0,25 liter/litres

Preserve 12 oz
Honigdose 0,35 liter
confiturier 0,35 litres

Jug 1 pint : 10 oz : 8 oz
Milchgiesser 0,5 : 0,35 : 0,25 ter
pot à lait 0,5 : 0,35 : 0,25 litre

Oval Baker 12 inch
Backplatte oval 30 cm
plat ovale à gratin 30 cm

Fruit Nappie 7 oz
Schälchen rund 0,20 liter 11,5 cm
bol rond 0,20 litres 11,5 cm

Soup Stand 6 inch
Untertasse 15 cm
soustasse 15 cm

Covered Sugar 8 oz
Zuckerdose m/D. 0,25 liter
sucrier avec couvercle 0,25 litres

Open Sugar 8 oz
Zuckerschale 0,25 liter 9 cm
bol à sucre 0,25 litres 9 cm

Purbeck Pottery Ltd., Seamoor Road, Bournemouth, BH4 9AQ, England

Stand 6 inch
Untersatz 15 cm
Dessous 15 cm

Soup/cereal/bowl lid

Pie dish/vegetable dish lid

Fruit dish/ice cream

Coaster 5 ins
Butter/jam dish 4 ins.

Butter pat

Egg cup 1½ ins.
Mustard 2½ ins.

Large soup 20 oz.
Soup/cereal 15 oz.

Vegetable/salad dish 3 pint.

Jug 1 pint
Jug ½ pint
Jug 8 oz

Oil/vinegar bottle

Spaghetti/salad bowl

Plate 10 ins.
Plate 8½ ins.
Plate 7 ins.
Chop dish 12 ins.

Oval steak plate 12 ins.
Oval steak plate 10¼ ins.

Salt/pepper
3 ins.

Salt/pepper
5 ins.

Salt/pepper
3 ins.

Lugged soup 15 oz.

Sauce Boat

Jug 1 pint
Jug ½ pint

Jug (Rondo)
1 litre ½ litre

74

FURTHER INFORMATION REQUEST

The authors are actively seeking further information with regard to Purbeck pottery. Any assistance will be gratefully received.

Plate 10, 8½, 7 inch
Teller flach 25, 21, 18 cm
assiette plate 25, 21, 18 cm

Goblet 6 oz.

Mug ½ pint
Beaker 7 oz

Mug ½ pint
Beaker 7 oz
Cup 9 oz
Cup 7 oz

Casserole 4 pint
Kasserolle rund 2,00 liter
casserole ronde 2,00 litres

Fruit/Salad Server 8 inch/2½ pint
Salatschale rund 20 cm/1,25 liter
saladier rond 20 cm/1,25 litres

Teapot 2½ pint
Teekanne 1,20 liter
théière 1,20 litres

Coffee Pot 3 pint
Kaffeekanne 1,50 liter
cafetière 1,50 litres

Coaster 5 ins.
Butter/jam dish 4 ins.

Oil/vinegar bottle

Saucer 6ins.
Soup bowl stand

Lugged Soup. 12 oz
Suppentasse 0,35 liter
tasse à consommé 0,35

Cup 8 oz
Tasse 0.25 liter/litres

Eggcup
Eierbecher
Coquetier

Mug 12 oz
Becher m/Hkl. 0,35 liter
gobelet à anse 0,35 litres

Soup/Cereal 12 oz
Suppenbol 0,35 liter
bol à potage 0.35 li

Saucer 6 inch
Untertasse 15 cm
soustasse 15 cm

Chop Dish 12 inch
Platte rund 30 cm
plat rond 30 cm

Oval butter dish

Salt and Pepper
Salz & Pfeffer
Sel & Poivre

Onion Soup 12 oz
Butterpfännchen 0,35 liter
caquelon à beurre 0,35 litres

Sauce boat ½ pint
Saucière 0,25 liter/litres

Preserve 12 oz
Honigdose 0,35 liter
confiturier 0,35 litres

Jug 1 pint : 10 oz : 8 oz
Milchgiesser 0,5 : 0,35 : 0,25 ter
pot à lait 0.5 : 0,35 : 0,25 litre

Oval Baker 12 inch
Backplatte oval 30 cm
plat ovale à gratin 30 cm

Fruit Nappie 7 oz
Schälchen rund 0,20 liter 11,5 cm
bol rond 0,20 litres 11,5 cm

Soup Stand 6 inch
Untertasse 15 cm
soustasse 15 cm

Covered Sugar 8 oz
Zuckerdose m/D. 0,25 liter
sucrier avec couvercle 0.25 litres

Open Sugar 8
Zuckerschale
bol à sucre 0,

Stand 6 inch
Untersatz 15 cm
Dessous 15 cm

Soup/cereal/bowl lid

Pie dish/vegetable dish lid

Purbeck Pottery Ltd., Seamoor Road, Bournemouth, BH4 9AQ, England

Fruit dish/ice cream

Coaster 5
Butter/jam dis

Butter pat

Egg cup 1½ ins.
Mustard 2½ ins.

Large soup 20 oz.
Soup/cereal 15 oz.

Vegetable/salad dish 3 pint.

Jug 1 pint
Jug ½ pint
Jug 8 oz.

Oil/vinegar bottle

Plate 10 ins
Plate 8½ ins.
Plate 7 ins.
Chop dish 12 ins.

Oval steak plate 12 ins.
Oval steak plate 10¼ ins.

Salt/pepper
3 ins.

Salt/pepper
5 ins.

Salt/pepper
3 ins.

Lugged soup 15 oz.

Sauce Boat

Spaghetti/salad bowl

Jug 1 pint
Jug ½ pint

Jug (Ro
li

CONTACT DETAILS:

email: alanpeat@tiscali.co.uk

address: Alan Peat (Purbeck Info.),
2 The Walled Garden
Grange Park Drive
Biddulph
Staffordshire
ST8 7TA

Plate 10, 8½, 7 inch
Teller flach 25, 21, 18 cm
assiette plate 25, 21, 18 cm

Goblet 6 oz.

Casserole 4 pint
Kasserolle rund 2,00 liter
casserole ronde 2,00 litres

Mug ½ pint
Beaker 7 oz

Fruit/Salad Server 8 inch/2½ pint
Salatschale rund 20 cm/1,25 liter
saladier rond 20 cm/1,25 litres

Mug ½ pint
Beaker 7 oz
Cup 9 oz.
Cup 7 oz.

Teapot 2¼ pint
Teekanne 1,20 liter
théière 1,20 litres

Coaster 5 ins
Butter/jam dish 4 ins.

Coffee Pot 3 pint
Kaffeekanne 1,50 liter
cafetière 1,50 litres

Cup 8 oz
Tasse 0,25 liter/litres

Oil/vinegar bottle

Eggcup
Eierbecher
Coquetier

Saucer 6ins.
Soup bowl stand

Mug 12 oz
Becher m/Hkl. 0,35 liter
gobelet à anse 0,35 litres

Lugged Soup 12 oz
Suppentasse 0,35 liter 11,5 cm
tasse à consommé 0,35 litres 11,5 cm

Soup/Cereal 12 oz
Suppenbol 0,35 liter 11,5 cm
bol à potage 0,35 litres 11,5 cm

Chop Dish 12 inch
Platte rund 30 cm
plat rond 30 cm

Saucer 6 inch
Untertasse 15 cm
soustasse 15 cm

Oval butter dish

Salt and Pepper
Salz & Pfeffer
Sel & Poivre

Onion Soup 12 oz
Butterpfännchen 0,35 liter
caquelon à beurre 0,35 litres

Sauce boat ½ pint
Saucière 0,25 liter/litres

Preserve 12 oz
Honigdose 0,35 liter
confiturier 0,35 litres

Jug 1 pint : 10 oz : 8 oz
Milchgiesser 0,5 : 0,35 : 0,25 ter
pot à lait 0,5 : 0,35 : 0,25 litre

Oval Baker 12 inch
Backplatte oval 30 cm
plat ovale à gratin 30 cm

Fruit Nappie 7 oz
Schälchen rund 0,20 liter 11,5 cm
bol rond 0,20 litres 11,5 cm

Soup Stand 6 inch
Untertasse 15 cm
soustasse 15 cm

Covered Sugar 8 oz
Zuckerdose m/D. 0,25 liter
sucrier avec couvercle 0,25 litres

Open Sugar 8 oz
Zuckerschale 0,25 liter 9 cm
bol à sucre 0,25 litres 9 cm

Stand 6 inch
Untersatz 15 cm
Dessous 15 cm

Soup/cereal/bowl lid

Pie dish/vegetable dish lid

Purbeck Pottery Ltd., Seamoor Road, Bournemouth, BH4 9AQ, England

Butter pat

Egg cup 1½ ins.
Mustard 2½ ins.

Large soup 20 oz
Soup/cereal 15 oz.

Vegetable/salad dish 3 pint.

Fruit dish/ice cream

Jug 1 pint
Jug ½ pint
Jug 8 oz.

Oil/vinegar bottle

Coaster 5 ins
Butter/jam dish 4 ins.

Plate 10 ins
Plate 8½ ins.
Plate 7 ins.
Chop dish 12 ins

Oval steak plate 12 ins.
Oval steak plate 10¼ ins.

Salt/pepper
3 ins.

Salt/pepper
5 ins.

Salt/pepper
3 ins.

Lugged soup 15 oz.

Sauce Boat
1 pint

Spaghetti/salad bowl

Mug ½ pint
Beaker 7oz

Butter dish lid

Jug 1 pint
Jug ½ pint
Jug 8 oz.

Jug (Rondo)
1 litre, ½ litre
¼ litre, 125ml

Goblet 6 oz.

Mug ½ pint
Beaker 7 oz

Mug ½ pint
Beaker 7 oz
Cup 9 oz.
Cup 7 oz.

Coaster 5 ins
Butter/jam dish 4 ins.

Oil/vinegar bottle

Saucer 6ins.
Soup bowl stand

Lugged Soup 12 oz
Suppentasse 0,35 liter
tasse à consommé 0,35

Plate 10, 8½, 7 inch
Teller flach 25, 21, 18 cm
assiette plate 25, 21, 18 cm

Casserole 4 pint
Kasserolle rund 2,00 liter
casserole ronde 2,00 litres

Fruit/Salad Server 8 inch/2½ pint
Salatschale rund 20 cm/1,25 liter
saladier rond 20 cm/1,25 litres

Teapot 2¼ pint
Teekanne 1,20 liter
théière 1,20 litres

Coffee Pot 3 pint
Kaffeekanne 1,50 liter
cafetière 1,50 litres

Cup 8 oz
Tasse 0,25 liter/litres

Eggcup
Eierbecher
Coquetier

Mug 12 oz
Becher m/Hkl. 0,35 liter
gobelet à anse 0,35 litres

Soup/Cereal 12 oz
Suppenbol 0,35 liter
bol à potage 0.35 lit

Chop Dish 12 inch
Platte rund 30 cm
plat rond 30 cm

Saucer 6 inch
Untertasse 15 cm
soustasse 15 cm

Oval butter dish

Salt and Pepper
Salz & Pfeffer
Sel & Poivre

Onion Soup 12 oz
Butterpfännchen 0,35 liter
caquelon à beurre 0,35 litres

Sauce boat ½ pint
Saucière 0,25 liter/litres

Preserve 12 oz
Honigdose 0,35 liter
confiturier 0.35 litres

Jug 1 pint : 10 oz : 8 oz
Milchgiesser 0,5 : 0,35 : 0,25 ter
pot à lait 0,5 : 0,35 : 0,25 litre

Oval Baker 12 inch
Backplatte oval 30 cm
plat ovale à gratin 30 cm

Fruit Nappie 7 oz
Schälchen rund 0,20 liter 11,5 cm
bol rond 0,20 litres 11,5 cm

Soup Stand 6 inch
Untertasse 15 cm
soustasse 15 cm

Covered Sugar 8 oz
Zuckerdose m/D. 0,25 liter
sucrier avec couvercle 0.25 litres

Open Sugar 8
Zuckerschale 0,2
bol à sucre 0,2

Stand 6 inch
Untersatz 15 cm
Dessous 15 cm

Butter pat

Soup/cereal/bowl lid

Pie dish/vegetable dish lid

Purbeck Pottery Ltd., Seamoor Road, Bournemouth, BH4 9AQ, England

Coaster 5 i
Butter/jam dish

Egg cup 1½ ins.
Mustard 2½ ins.

Fruit dish/ice cream

Large soup 20 oz.
Soup/cereal 15 oz.

Vegetable/salad dish 3 pint.

Jug 1 pint
Jug ½ pint
Jug 8 oz.

Oil/vinegar bottle

Plate 10 ins
Plate 8½ ins.
Plate 7 ins.
Chop dish 12 ins.

Oval steak plate 12 ins.
Oval steak plate 10¼ ins.

Spaghetti/salad bowl

Salt/pepper
3 ins.

Salt/pepper
5 ins.

Salt/pepper
3 ins.

Lugged soup 15 oz.

Sauce Boat
1 pint

Mug ½ pint
Beaker 7oz

Butter dish lid

Jug 1 pint
Jug ½ pint
Jug 8 oz.

Jug (Rondo
1 litre, ½ litre
¼ litre, 125

DEDICATION

Our thanks are due to all past and present members of Purbeck Pottery who assisted in the research for this book. Thanks also to Julie Peat for editing the text, Glyn Matthews for the photography, Simon Matthews for all the design work and Angela Burt for proofreading.

Alan Peat and Pete Freeman 2011